INTERNATIONAL

Science
Foundation Plus
Activity Book C

Published by Collins
An imprint of HarperCollins*Publishers*
The News Building, 1 London Bridge Street,
London, SE1 9GF, UK

HarperCollins Publishers
Macken House, 39/40 Mayor Street Upper,
Dublin 1, D01 C9W8, Ireland

Browse the complete Collins catalogue at
www.collins.co.uk

ISBN 978-0-00-846875-0

British Library Cataloguing-in-Publication Data
A catalogue record for this publication is available from the British Library.

Author: Fiona Macgregor
Publisher: Elaine Higgleton
Product manager: Letitia Luff
Commissioning editor: Rachel Houghton
Researcher: Andi Colombo
Edited by: Eleanor Barber
Editorial management: Oriel Square
Cover designer: Kevin Robbins
Cover illustrations: Jouve India Pvt Ltd.
Internal illustrations: Jouve India Pvt. Ltd.; p10, p 14 Tasneem Amiruddin,
p 22b Nathalie Ortega
Typesetter: Jouve India Pvt. Ltd.
Production controller: Lyndsey Rogers
Printed in India by Multivista Global Pvt. Ltd.

Acknowledgements

With thanks to all the kindergarten staff and their schools around the world who
have helped with the development of this course, by sharing insights and
commenting on and testing sample materials:

Calcutta International School: Sharmila Majumdar, Mrs Pratima Nayar, Preeti
Roychoudhury, Tinku Yadav, Lakshmi Khanna, Mousumi Guha, Radhika Dhanuka,
Archana Tiwari, Urmita Das; Gateway College (Sri Lanka): Kousala Benedict; Hawar
International School: Kareen Barakat, Shahla Mohammed, Jennah Hussain; Manthan
International School: Shalini Reddy; Monterey Pre-Primary: Adina Oram; Prometheus
School: Aneesha Sahni, Deepa Nanda; Pragyanam School: Monika Sachdev; Rosary
Sisters High School: Samar Sabat, Sireen Freij, Hiba Mousa; Solitaire Global School:
Devi Nimmagadda; United Charter Schools (UCS): Tabassum Murtaza; Vietnam
Australia International School: Holly Simpson

The publishers wish to thank the following for permission to reproduce photographs.

(t = top, c = centre, b = bottom, r = right, l = left)

p 22c1 Tim Platt. All other photographs: Shutterstock.

MIX
Paper | Supporting
responsible forestry
FSC™ C007454

This book contains FSC™ certified paper and other controlled
sources to ensure responsible forest management.

For more information visit: www.harpercollins.co.uk/green

Colour

1 Day

2 Night

1 Colour the weather during the day.
2 Colour the weather at night.

Date:

Try this

1

2

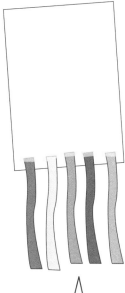

3

4

Follow the instructions to make a windsock.

Date:

Draw

Day 1	
Day 2	
Day 3	
Day 4	
Day 5	

Draw the weather each school day this week.

sunny   cloudy   rainy

windy   foggy   hot ●   cold ●   Date:

Draw

1	2
3	4

Watch a cotton wool 'cloud' experiment.
Draw what happened next.

Date:

Find

Which things are made of wood? Colour in everything that is made of wood. Which things are made of glass? Which things are made of metal? Date:

Tick

	Hard	Soft
cotton wool		
book		
cardboard		
paper clip		
ruler		
cloth		

Tick to show whether each object is hard or soft.

Date:

Match

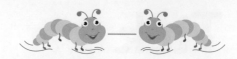

jumper

ring

door

Match the objects and the materials.

Date:

Count and colour

PCM 18. Colour in a block for each object.
Count the blocks and write the number.   Date:

Cross out

Cross out all the litter.

Date:

Draw

Draw four pieces of litter that you saw on your walk.

Date:

Say and colour

plastic	metal	glass	food

What types of litter did you see on the walk?
Colour in one block for each piece of litter you saw.   Date:

Sort

Recycle	Rubbish

PCM 19. Cut out the pictures. Stick the things you can recycle in the green box. Stick the rubbish in the yellow box.

Date:

Circle

push / pull

push / pull

push / pull

push / pull

Push or pull? Circle the correct word for each picture.

Date:

Cut and stick

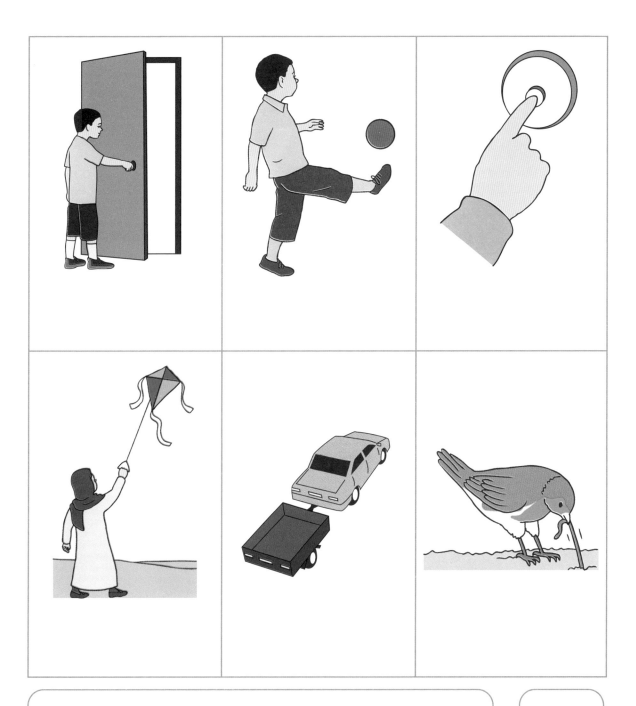

PCM 20. Push or pull? Cut out and stick the
correct word for each picture.   Date:

Trace and say

push

pull

Trace and say the words.

Date:

Draw

	☺	☹
pin		
paper clip		
ruler		
glue		
book		

Use your magnet. Draw ☺ if the magnet pulls the object.
Draw ☹ if it doesn't.   Date:

Find out

	balloon	play-dough	paper clip	paper
bend				
stretch				
squash				
twist				
change back?				

Try the actions with the objects. Tick the boxes.

Date:

Tick and say

butter		chocolate	
Yes ☐		Yes ☐	
No ☐		No ☐	

ice		rock	
Yes ☐		Yes ☐	
No ☐		No ☐	

metal		wood	
Yes ☐		Yes ☐	
No ☐		No ☐	

candle wax		sugar	
Yes ☐		Yes ☐	
No ☐		No ☐	

Tick the box if the material melts.

Date:

☐

Tick and say

	Yes ☐ No ☐		Yes ☐ No ☐
	Yes ☐ No ☐		Yes ☐ No ☐
	Yes ☐ No ☐		Yes ☐ No ☐
	Yes ☐ No ☐		Yes ☐ No ☐
	Yes ☐ No ☐		Yes ☐ No ☐

Tick the box if you think it will burn.

Date:

Match

cook

cut

burn

melt

Draw lines to match the pictures
with the correct description.

Date:

Match

Revie

We use materials.

It is raining.

Pick up the mess.

She is pulling.

Match the sentences to the pictures.

Date:

Review

Tick

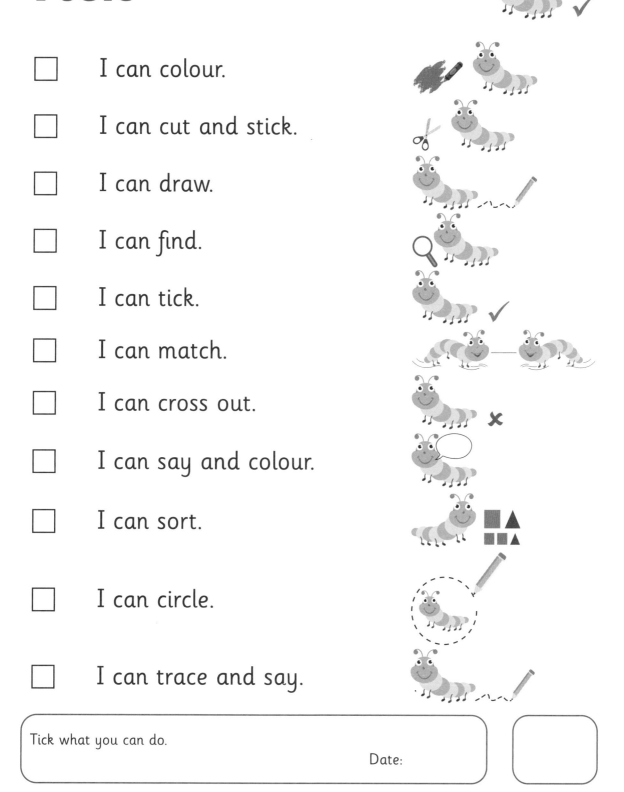

☐   I can colour.

☐   I can cut and stick.

☐   I can draw.

☐   I can find.

☐   I can tick.

☐   I can match.

☐   I can cross out.

☐   I can say and colour.

☐   I can sort.

☐   I can circle.

☐   I can trace and say.

Tick what you can do.

Date:

Assessment record

_____ has achieved these Science Foundation Plus Phase Objectives:

Know that wind is moving air	1	2	3
Know that rain falls to Earth from clouds	1	2	3
Observe and record weather over time	1	2	3
Describe physical properties of some materials	1	2	3
Sort and group materials using one criterion and record observations	1	2	3
Investigate and record types of litter at school	1	2	3
Understand that waste has to be disposed of and that some waste can be recycled	1	2	3
Explore and describe how pushes and pulls can make familiar everyday objects move	1	2	3
Play with magnets to explore their properties	1	2	3
Explore and notice what happens when magnets touch different materials	1	2	3
Explore how familiar materials can change and understand that some of these changes can be undone	1	2	3

1: Partially achieved
2: Achieved
3: Exceeded

Signed by teacher:
Signed by parent: Date: